Digital Photography Tips

By Raj Vitthalpura

This book tribute to my younger brother *Dipak Vitthalpura*, who give me a chance to publish this book..

Thank you and I glad to my dear brother Dipu..

-Raj Vitthalpura

Digital VS. Film

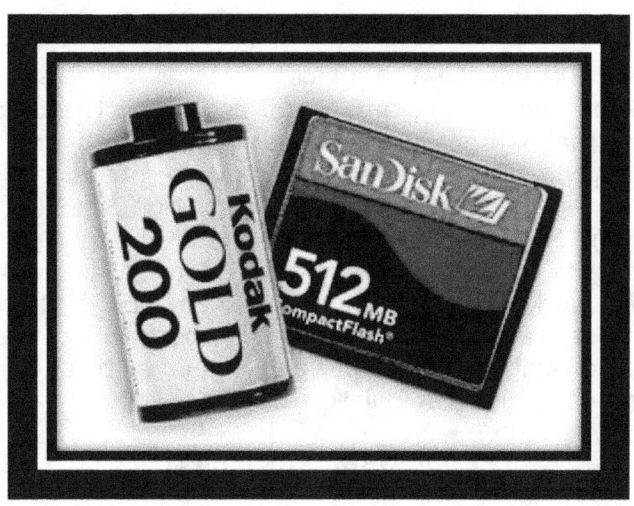

The debate between digital cameras and film cameras is relatively new – digital photography itself has only in the past few years made it to the point where it could rival film, and most agree that it has finally met (if not surpassed) its rival in ease and flexibility. The range of camera choices above 3 megapixels (which is comparable to good quality point and shoot cameras, and will provide acceptable snapshots) is very wide, while 5-10 megapixel cameras or greater are available near the top of almost every camera line for excellent quality results. Professional quality digital SLR camera are available that will provide greater than 20 megapixel images, and are generally only necessary if you are looking for significant enlargements, or require the highest quality and detail for commercial photography.

Quality differences

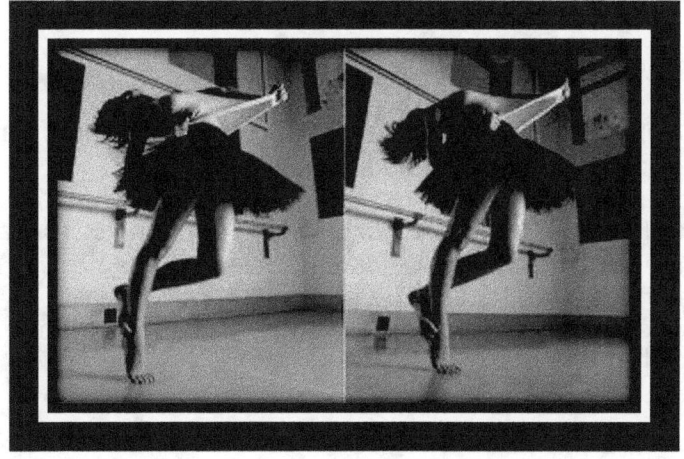

The results are similar from both film and digital cameras, especially in the case of outdoor shots where the difference can be almost indistinguishable between the two. With low light levels indoors, photos taken with both types of cameras can be susceptible to granularity or artifacts, however most users don't notice the effects - and many software applications exist that can reduce the artifacts, whether from a digital camera or from a film print that is scanned in. Ultimately, the camera industry has taken the tools to a point where even though the canvas has changed, the quality is similar - so the decision can be made by the artist whether they want film or digital, with many now choosing digital because of the inherent flexibility.

Film quality also relates primarily to the quality of the lens and the film, where digital camera quality is also impacted by the amount of resolution the camera is capable of, and the in-camera processing that is done when a shot is taken – prior to even taking a picture, you will know whether your digital camera is capable of taking pictures that can be displayed/printed in larger sizes (the higher the resolution, the larger prints that can be made at a similar quality). Many higher-end cameras also allow pictures to be taken in a 'raw' format, which bypasses the image processing done in the camera - this requires the photographer to do more work after the photo is taken, but it provides more control over the final image. In contrast, taking a photo with film permanently records it based on the conditions at the time (including choices between colour or black and white), although film images can always be scanned and manipulated later.

Advantages of digital

Some of the main advantages to digital photography are:

- the ability to easily preview pictures and delete any bad shots, and know immediately if a particular photo needs to be re-shot
- the costs of film are replaced with memory cards/sticks that can be re-used again and again, with the larger cards/sticks having a capacity of thousands of pictures
- since pictures are saved on memory cards/sticks, you can easily share pictures by copying off the photos, or sharing the card/stick
- decisions on effects like cropping, sepia tones or black and white, can be easily made after the picture has already been taken

Choosing Camera

Certainly, the most obvious question that users have is what kind of camera they should choose. Camera users normally fall into one of three main categories: amateurs, hobbyists and professionals, and knowing where you fit can help you identify what features might be important, and what type of camera would make sense for your needs. Are you looking to just take a few pictures of family and friends, capture memories from vacations, or produce shots of nature and landscapes to build a portfolio? Also think about how much quality you are willing to trade away for portability, as cameras can range from large and bulky professional quality SLR cameras (Single Lens Reflex) to small ultra-portable cameras, some of which may not even have a flash.

Camera categories

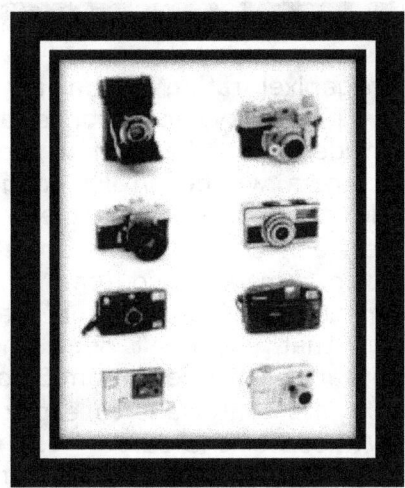

Cameras are typically broken down into groups: ultra-compact, compact, prosumer or hobbyist, and digital SLR, and most manufacturers build units in several categories to capture more of the market. On each end of the range, the ultra-compacts are designed to be the most portable, often fitting into pockets easily and used as key chains, while the digital SLR cameras are professional quality tools that have the widest range of options, such as external flashes, lenses and tripods (but are also often the largest and most cumbersome to carry). Most units fall into the middle two categories, with compacts having a good range of quality, resolution, and options, and the prosumer range including higher quality and greater control over manual options and accessories.

Megapixels

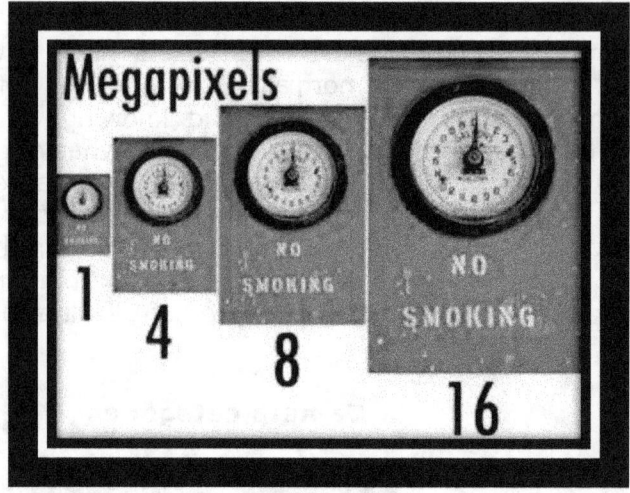

Buying by only the megapixel rating will mean you will miss out on the other features of the camera – portability, accessories, a good quality flash, but it is one of the most important considerations. Less than 3 megapixel cameras are suitable for basic snapshots; the camera will be small and good enough to take basic 'I was there' shots, but the images won't be as clear if you want anything larger than standard 4x6 prints. Between 3 and 5 megapixels, you will find a good range of everyday use and vacation cameras – you can fill your photo albums with shots from cameras in this range or use them as desktop images, as you will generally find the images are good enough that you don't need any more and will be able to make good quality prints at a variety of sizes. From 5 to 10 megapixels, you will find more serious cameras for hobbyists that want to explore photography as an art or those that are looking to stay ahead of the curve – the images will take up more hard drive space but will be perfect for manipulation and printing out in larger sizes. A number of cameras are available across different categories with 10 megapixels or more, although this kind of resolution is generally overkill for casual everyday use. Choose a 10 megapixel or higher resolution camera if you are a professional and expect to be paid for the work you produce, if you need the highest resolution because you expect to make significant enlargements of your photos for mounting/framing, if you want more flexible cropping options, or if you simply want the ultimate in image quality.

Zoom

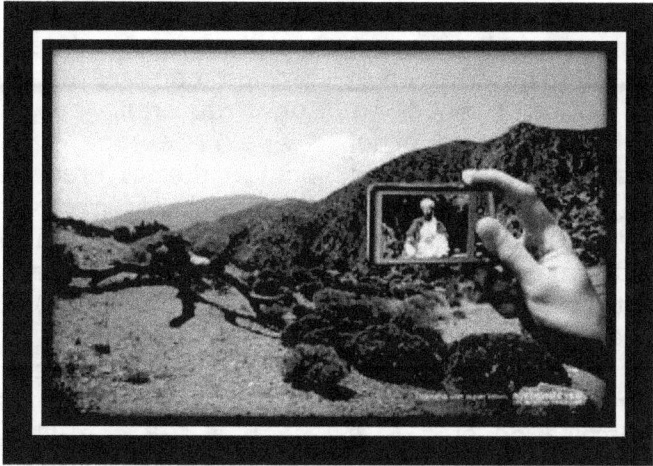

Zooming is another important consideration with digital cameras - there are two kinds of zoom: optical zoom and digital zoom. An optical zoom factor is one that relies on the lens itself magnifying the light coming in, so that what is distant appears larger and closer in the resulting image. A digital zoom factor is one that takes the resulting image and magnifies it after the fact. Needless to say, an optical zoom factor is much more important than a digital zoom factor (and produces better quality results).

Storage media

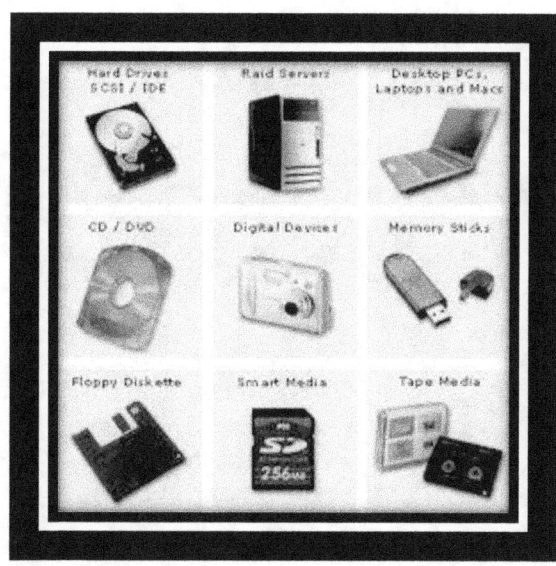

The way the images themselves are stored can be a factor in your decision, as some camera makers have proprietary storage systems that are incompatible with the cameras of other makes. Some common formats are Compact Flash (a fairly common format across both compact and professional cameras), Secure Digital (SD) cards (which are fairly common in compact cameras due to their smaller size), and Sony Memory Stick (unique to Sony cameras, but also supported by Sony computers, televisions, and other devices). Storage sizes can range from smaller 8MB cards/sticks, which can hold about a dozen three megapixel images, to larger 32GB cards/sticks and higher, which can hold thousands of images, and are especially useful when storing photos in a 'raw' format (a direct unprocessed copy of the image data from the camera sensor, available more commonly with digital SLR cameras, and takes much more storage space per photo). Prices have come down on most of the memory cards/sticks making selection of the larger sizes more affordable and a smarter choice. Choose the largest size you are comfortable with, and ideally select a second smaller stick as a backup in case the first one becomes full – for example, a combination of a 512MB with a 4GB card/stick is good if you move all your images onto your computer on a regular basis.

Accessories

A problem many people have is that you never know what you'll run into – when vacationing in southern Europe, it is likely already too late to remember that you needed an extra memory card/stick, a spare battery, or can't take a picture that doesn't shake like Jello. This is where accessories come in – they can help to complete a picture-taking experience by giving the one thing you didn't know you needed so you can get the perfect shot or the job done.

Carrying case

Perhaps the accessory that gets the least respect by amateur photographers is a carrying case or bag. Ironically, this is the easiest way to not only protect your investment, which can easily cost up to or over $1000, but to also bring along all the spare parts you may or may not need on that particular day. With extra pockets, slots and a good solid strap, you can make sure you haven't left anything behind and can still keep your hands free when trekking around on a mountain. Of course, it's also the easiest way to identify a tourist in a foreign land, but everything has trade-offs.

Tripod

Tripods are commonly used to minimize tremor associated with night shots, long zooms or professional portraits where as much time is spent organizing the audience rather than simply capturing a scene. For the budget- or space-conscious, buy a fist-sized beanbag or hacky sack and bring it with you – it makes a very flexible mini-tripod. Even some professionals will use them in awkward situations, like positioning the camera on a rock, ledge or other precarious positions. The moldable shape and portability make it the perfect must-have accessory.

Additional lenses

Lenses are often overlooked by all but professionals and serious hobbyists, but they do have applications with the lucky owner whose camera allows for those upgrades. Wide-angle lenses and telephoto lenses can be used well in nature scenes, conjuring up visions of the Grand Canyon or safaris along the Serengeti. Filters are inserted in front of the lens itself and distort or affect the light coming through to the camera's light sensor. A polarizing filter, or polarizer, for example, filters light as it angles further away from straight ahead, and as a result gives truer tones to objects in its field of vision - which really helps to take the glare off of sunny days. In many cases, these effects can be reproduced with software programs that crop an image, tweak the colour spectrum, and otherwise alter the image, however, generally speaking, the less editing you have to do of your pictures after the fact, the easier photography will be for you.

Other accessories

When traveling or just heading away from home for an afternoon, plan on having a travel pack of accessories: additional batteries or a charger in case your camera battery dies on you, an external flash, and an extra memory card/stick or two in case you run out of room (many photographers find a good mix with large, medium, and small sizes a good fit – the large card/stick is the main storage used 95% of the time, the medium serving as backup with enough space to hold a day's worth of pictures, and the small card/stick big enough for half a dozen shots in an emergency).

Taking Photos

Proper handling of the camera itself can reduce the number of retakes, helping to make your day easier by decreasing the number of times you need to repeat the dreaded "hold on, I need to take one more". Taking better quality pictures means taking fewer pictures overall since you're taking fewer bad shots due to bad mechanics.

Holding the camera

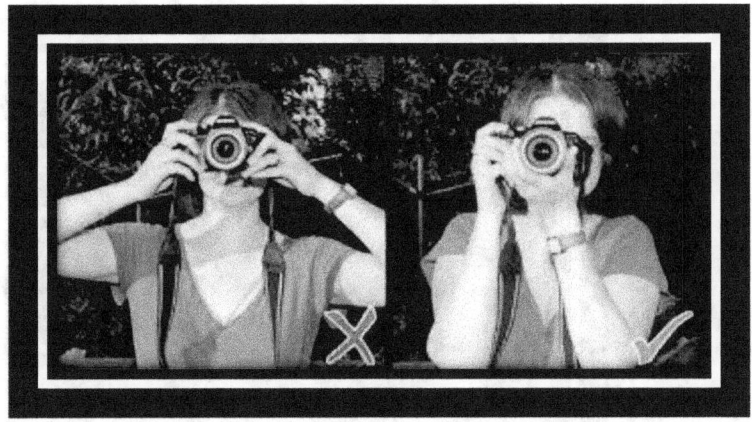

Hold the camera solidly in your hand to prevent the camera from shuddering or shifting too much when pressing on the shutter button, and watch your spare fingers so that they don't interfere with the lens. One trick is to wrap the camera strap around your fingers so that you will be more conscious of where they are. Another tip, especially with smaller cameras, is to hold your eye up to the optical viewfinder to capture the image, rather than the electronic viewfinder – this will not only help you see exactly what your capturing, but will also help to stabilize the shot between your hands and your face for less 'camera shake'.

Focusing

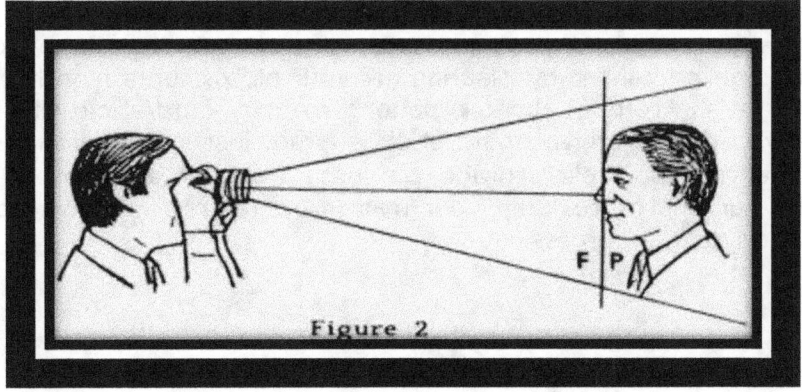

Figure 2

As digital cameras have a tendency to take slightly longer to focus than film camera, an important tip is to half-depress the shutter button until the camera has had time to lock the focus, and then completely press the button to take the actual shot - this can often make the difference between blurry, out-of-focus shots, and clear pictures. Also, with normal picture-taking, shutter speeds are fast enough that a small amount of shake won't affect the resulting image much, however, there are times when you'd want to use a tripod to compensate: when taking pictures in low light, where the shutter speed will slow down enough to potentially make drag lines, and when using a long zoom, where distant objects are susceptible to blur. In each case, the tripod will settle the image and let you forget about shaking the image and focus on capturing what's in your mind's eye.

Preview

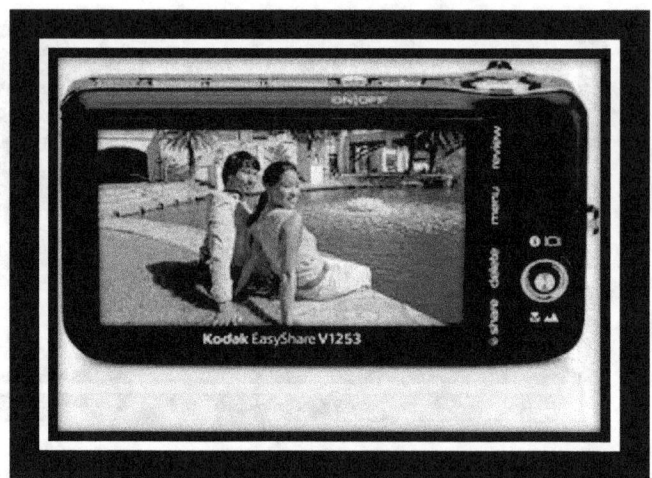

One of the main advantages of a digital camera is being able to preview the pictures after you've taken them. If you are trying to capture a specific scene, you can review the shot and see if it looks the way you wanted – if it doesn't, you can delete the shot and retake it to get it right. Why keep a picture if it's blurry, or someone's eyes are closed, or a person is obstructing part of the view?

Archiving

Taking that one step further, there is no worse feeling than seeing the perfect kiss, smile or sunset, reaching for your camera and clicking the button, only to realize that your storage is full and you've missed your chance. It's happened to everyone, but still, you can prevent it by clearing off your old pictures monthly (or more frequently if you are a shutterbug). Bring a second memory card/stick with you when you go on a trip, even if your primary card/stick is large, just in case you need the extra space. There are also portable storage products available that allow you to offload and archive your photos to keep your main storage free, ranging from iPod adapters to portable drives/CD burners.

Composition

Many people comment on certain photographers having an eye for taking good pictures. In part, that is skill and experience you are seeing. Another part is the expression of art with an understanding of some basic rules. Of course, like any artist, you can take some great shots that 'break' all the rules, however, it is safe to say that taking into consideration the following six items will help improve the quality of your pictures and create more interesting images.

keep it simple

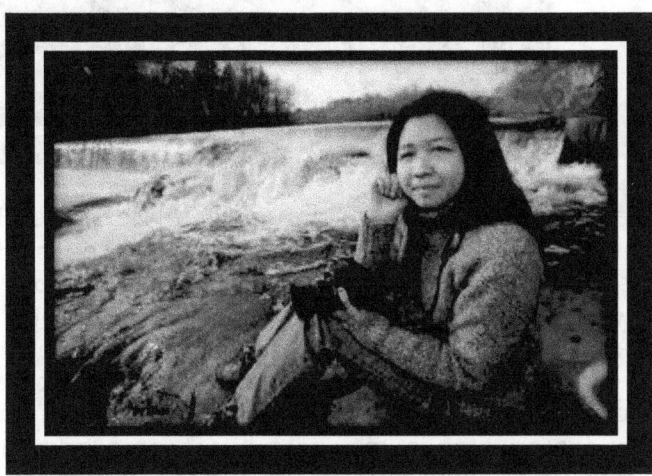

Think to yourself, "What am I taking a picture of?" and keep that in mind. Identifying the subject of interest and avoiding distracting backgrounds will help to keep the picture clear. Zoom in to clear out irrelevant parts of the scene and capture just what you're looking for, avoiding objects like signs, buildings or people that take the viewer's eye away from the point of focus. An example of this is taking a picture of crowd of protestors - a busy image where the eye has trouble figuring out what should take its focus. Zooming in on one protestor in particular, though, makes it very clear what should command the viewer's attention.

Rule of thirds

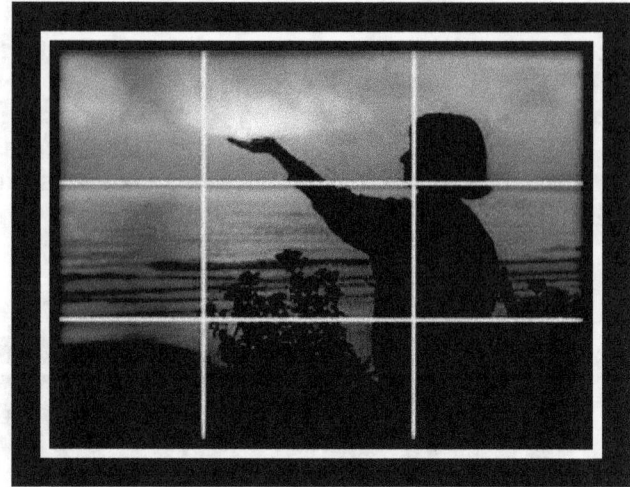

Picture a tic tac toe board: two horizontal lines intersected by two vertical lines. This creates an easy formula - line up the horizon of the shot with either of the two horizontal lines, and line up the subject (either a person, building or the focus of your picture) with either of the vertical lines, ideally where the lines intersect. When viewing a scene, try to overlay this map into the viewfinder - with only a little adjustment, you can quickly create more visually interesting images by simply adjusting (or cropping after the fact) what you see to line up with these invisible markers. When dealing with a moving subject or a person, it's often preferable to have them looking or moving 'into' the picture from one of the two sides.

Lines and shapes

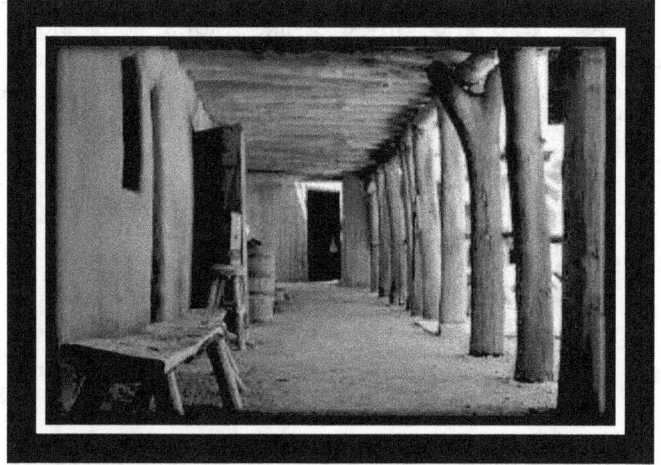

We all remember our geometry classes, dominated by circles, triangles, and snake-like curves. Applying these simple shapes to your subject matter can help to simplify complex scenes and add visual interest. Consider trying to capture an image of a person walking down a long, straight street. Instead of shooting straight down the line, move yourself five or ten feet to the side and shoot that road at an angle - having that line crossing through the intersecting lines of the imaginary tic tac toe board from the rule of thirds can create the illusion of movement as they lead the eye through the picture. S-curves are even more dynamic, while repetitive lines can also create movement of the eye through the picture, like repeating waves of sand on a beach or parallel row houses along the side of a road.

Vantage point

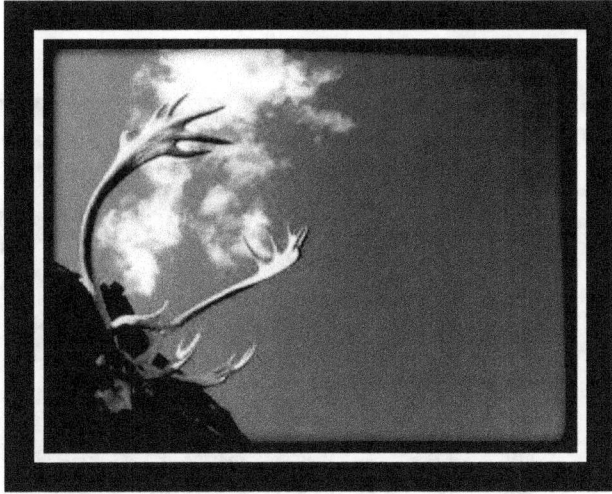

Most images taken by amateur photographers are taken at eye level - this means most of these pictures are taken from the narrow range of 5 to 6 feet in height. Taking a picture from a lower vantage point (for example crouching or even lying on the ground) can add grandeur and significance to the subject, while getting more height (from climbing up a tree, fence or steps) will reduce the significance of the subject in your scene. Examples of using this could be taking a picture of your children playing looking from the ground, or capturing a busy marketplace scene where no one person would stand out over another.

Balance

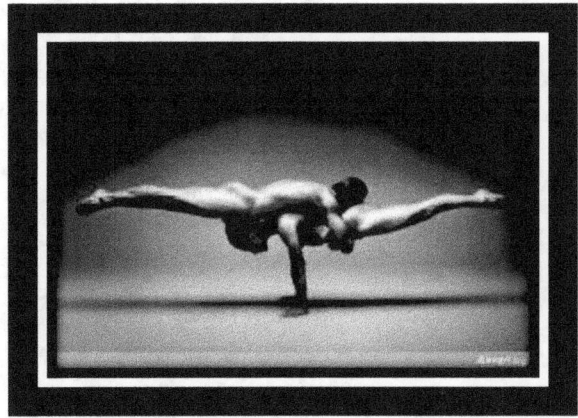

When considering what you're capturing, look through the lens and pick out the dominant subjects, like people, buildings, trees or mountains and arrange them so that they complement each other. This can mean either symmetrical balancing, where objects of equal size are positioned on either side of the picture's center, like a manicured garden with bushes on either side, or asymmetrical balancing, where objects of different sizes are used on either side of the picture's center, like a scene of a person standing between a house and a tree. Asymmetrical pictures are often more interesting and visually stimulating as the viewer's eye moves from object to object.

Framing

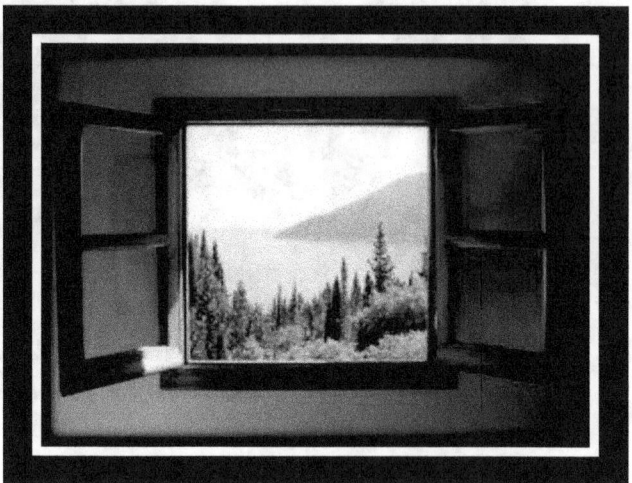

Framing, as it sounds, is a way of drawing attention to the subject in the picture by blocking off or framing parts of the scene using natural or artificial barriers, and however accomplished can add prominence to the subject, and will help add a sense of depth to the photo. Using this concept literally, you can try taking an outdoor scene from the inside through an open window to create interest, or capture a newly married couple kissing in a doorway or hallway to draw the eye to them. Other more natural ways of framing a shot are using trees (shooting through gaps in the branches and leaves), or viewing a beach from between craggy rocks.

Lighting

The most important thing to understand about photography, whether it's digital or film, is that it's all about capturing light. So by understanding how different light affects your picture, you can significantly change the way your pictures turn out. Ideally, whenever possible, ensure that there is enough ambient light - the light that is already available whether it's natural sunlight outdoors or indoor light fixtures. The more that is available, the easier it will be to take a picture without having to be concerned with aperture, shutter speed, or flashes.

Indoor photos

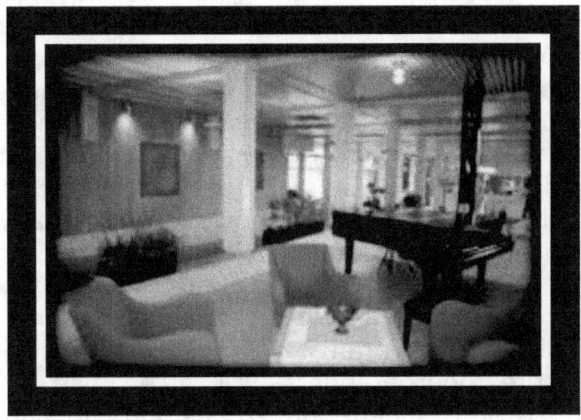

The most obvious area where this isn't always possible is indoors. No ceiling light or table lamp can be as bright as the sun, so you will almost always have to add more light with a flash. Most professional photographers prefer to have more control over the lighting so they will use a variety of stronger lights to help them. By adding more light to an indoor scene, you can avoid the need for a camera flash, which can be distracting to the subject, particularly when you are trying to capture unposed or natural shots.

Flash

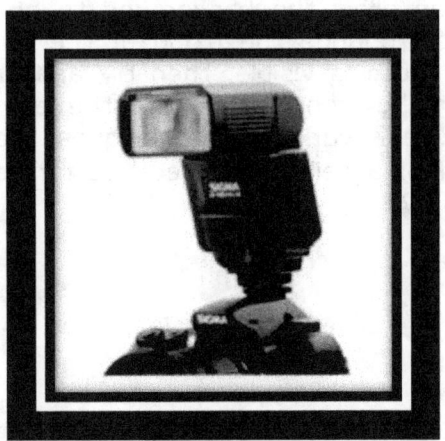

When it isn't practical to add more light to an indoor or low-light scene, you can often rely on a flash to help add to the available light. A common mistake with a flash, however, is to misunderstand the reach of the resulting light. Most portable cameras can only light up a subject within an average of 10 to 15 feet – so, if the subject of the photo is further away than that, then either move closer, or look for an alternate light source or option. Professional photographers will often use an external flash, which can be synchronized with the camera like a built-in flash, but can be much brighter, as well as having the ability to position it separately from the camera itself.

Camera adjustments

Where lighting is less than optimum, you also have a number of options at your disposal if your camera provides more manual control over its functions. Many of these options simply allow for more light to enter the camera (more depth into these features is discussed on the next page covering advanced techniques). By adjusting the aperture, you can widen the lens opening to let more light in at one time into the camera, thereby taking more of the existing light in than you would otherwise. You can also adjust the shutter speed – by using a longer shutter speed, you allow more time for the available light to enter, however the disadvantage of doing this is that your shots are more prone to camera shake and blurring, so be aware and mount the camera on a flat surface or use a tripod. Many cameras also offer the ability to adjust the exposure which can help to compensate for having either too much or too little light available. A more dramatic example of these kinds of adjustments is with night shots, where photographers will often use a combination of all three, sometimes with shutter speeds of 20 seconds or longer, to effectively capture nighttime traffic, starry galaxies, or unique images of popular monuments.

Controlled lighting

As you become more comfortable with lighting, you can change the feeling of a photo by controlling the way light hits different parts of the scene or subject. For example, having the light hit the side of a subject can add more contrast between facial features and shadows, making for a more dramatic pose. Having the light behind a subject can allow the background to be lit while the foreground is dark, which can completely change the mood of the photo. If you want to ensure that everything in your photo is visible, then try and ensure that the indoor or outdoor light is hitting from the front for the most even view of the scene. Many studio photographers will use a variety of techniques, including multiple light sources and bouncing a flash off of a ceiling or object, to further control the lighting of portraits and other staged scenes.

Advanced techniques

If your camera provides manual control over its functions, you can get a lot more control over the resulting image. The types of advanced techniques will be different depending on the type of camera you have – smaller point-and-shoot cameras typically will have fewer options (or limit the options to common presets), where more advanced cameras will bring greater flexibility of how the picture is taken, and prosumer and DSL cameras have lenses that allow for further creative picture taking options.

Aperture

Controlling the aperture is an advanced technique which allows you to control the width of the lens opening (like the iris of an eye), allowing for more direct control over how much light enters the camera, and is normally referred to as an 'F-stop' or 'aperture number' such as F2.8 or F8 (a higher number refers to a smaller aperture opening, which means it is letting in less light, and a smaller number refers to a larger aperture opening - in this case, F refers to the focal length of the lens). A smaller aperture number allows you to use a shorter shutter speed (which makes it better for fast action shots), while a larger aperture allows you to use a longer shutter when there is bright light (for example, capturing the motion of a waterfall on a sunny day). Controlling the aperture also affects the depth of field within the photo (which refers to how much of the photo is in focus at the same time). For example, with landscape photography, you could use a small aperature to get a greater depth of field and have the whole scene in focus to see all the details, however with portrait or macro photography, you can use a larger aperture to get a shallow depth of field and isolate/highlight the subject by forcing the rest of the photo out of focus (DOF is also affected by focal length - the longer the focal length the less DOF, so because most smaller compact cameras have shorter focal lengths, it can be difficult for them to achieve a shallow DOF).

Shutter speed

Controlling the shutter speed can also allow you to change the feel of a photo – for example, you may want a fast shutter speed to capture fast action, sports, or other areas where you'd want to 'freeze the scene' like a busy marketplace, or use a slower shutter speed to capture low light shots or introduce a sense of motion into the photo - for example, capturing the movement of water in a waterfall or traffic along a busy city street.

iso/exposure

In a parallel to the film camera world, digital cameras uses ISO to refer to the sensitivity of the digital sensor (in the same way that film ISO refers to the sensitivity of the film). ISO is referred to numerically, such as ISO 100 or ISO 800, with the higher value meaning more sensitive to exposure from light. Normally this is controlled automatically by the camera, but by manually changing the ISO value, you can make the camera sensor more sensitive to light, allowing you to take photos with a faster shutter speed (a shorter exposure), or with a longer exposure when working with low light. The trade-off of a higher ISO value is that it is similar to turning up the volume on a stereo when the recording is quiet - you hear the music louder, but you also hear more background noise. In the same way, using a higher ISO value will introduce more noise into the photo, although there are many noise-reduction software packages that will allow you to reduce or eliminate noise afterwards.

Filters/lenses

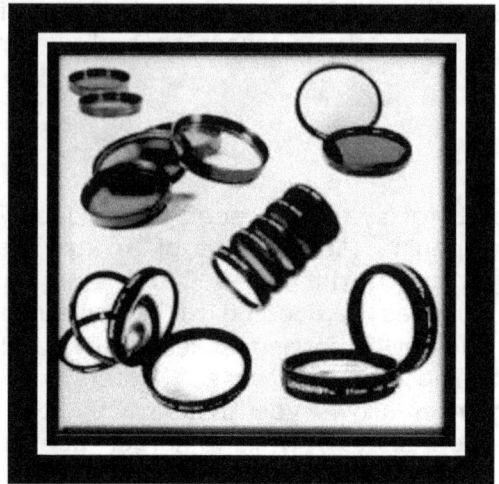

The use of filters or lenses can allow you to completely change how light hits the camera, for example, there are a number of add-on filters that can either soften the photo, provide slight blurring around the edges to capture a sensitive mood in portraits, add light flares for a touch of drama, or a polarizer which controls stray light and glare and provides richer, more vivid/saturated photos (if your camera doesn't support filters, one trick is to use a pair of polarizing sunglasses in front of the lens as a polarizing filter - for best results try shooting with the sun behind you). Additionally, more advanced cameras can allow you to add on lenses to the main fixed lens, or change the main lens out completely; in both cases, this can let you use a macro lens, which can help you to get closer to a subject than you otherwise would be able to, like an insect or flower, a wide angle lens for landscape shots and good for capturing landmarks or other large scenes, or a telephoto lens that can give you longer zooms than your camera allows to get closer to a distant object or subject, perfect for a safari trip.

Touching Up Photos

A major advantage of digital photography is being able to easily rewrite history – you can make changes to the photos before printing or displaying. There are a variety of software packages that will allow you to do this - some photo album software will allow simple touch ups, like Google's Picasa, Apple's iPhoto or LView, while more complex packages offer more diverse editing flexibility and more professional results, such as Adobe Photoshop, or Corel Paint Shop Pro. Most software packages offer inline help features and tutorials to guide you through these techniques and more.

Post-processing

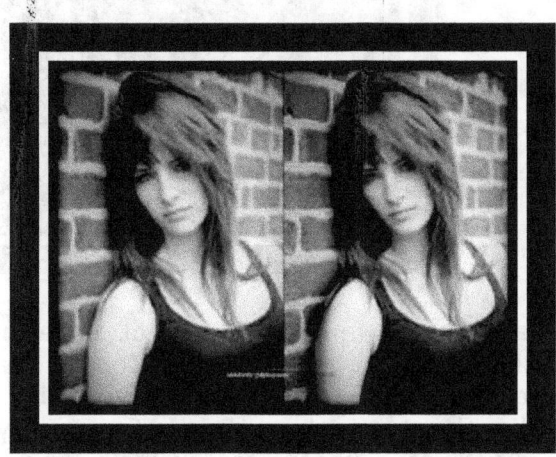

Common edits to photos include the elimination of red-eye, which many software packages can do with a simple click of a button, and the removal of an unwanted item from a scene, like a stray swimmer or unwanted car on the road – this is called cloning, where the software samples one section of the image to replace the other. By using parts of the original image, the colouring and texture are the same, so results are good enough to fool almost anybody. Another common touchup is to adjust the amount of light that was available when the photo was originally taken – literally, changing how bright some colours are in relation to others, and how bright the image looks overall. For example, this can make a dark photo look brighter, or a dull photo more vivid.

Adjusting the horizon

Another simple correction that can be made is to rotate the photo so that the horizon or objects captured appear straight. This is often more than simply rotating the image 90 degrees one way or the other, from portrait to landscape, but instead leveling the photo so that it looks straight. Because of the perspective of the photo, it may not be possible to make everything level at once, so you should use the horizon as your ruler, or take a dominant object in the scene, like a person or building, and use that as a guide.

Cropping

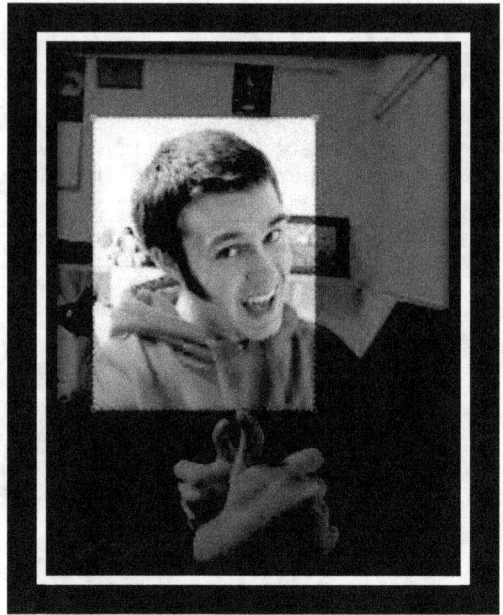

Cropping can be another powerful editing tool, especially with newer cameras that have greater resolution (giving you a larger source image to work from). Cropping trims off unwanted parts of the photo leaving you with the parts you want to keep. This can have a significant effect on the photo, since you can change the balance, composition and drama of a photo, for example, in a photo where a subject was centered, you can crop off more on one side to align objects with the rule of thirds, or remove portions of the background, like a building, tree or stray person. You can also crop a photo to change it from landscape to portrait, leading to a more interesting picture than the one you originally took.

Printing Photos

One by-product of the digital photography revolution is that photographers no longer need to rely on traditional film processing or darkrooms to enjoy their prints. Understanding the relationship between camera resolution and final print size can help you make decisions on what pictures are the best to print, and how to go about printing them. Normal snapshot prints can be made of images that are 2 to 3 megapixels, but you will normally require a higher resolution to print larger photographs.

Traditional printing

Fortunately, most traditional film photo printing services also provide printing services for digital camera users. To take advantage of these services, you have flexible options: drop off just your memory card or stick, bring in your whole camera, bring in a copy of your pictures on a CD - or submit them electronically over the Internet, bypassing the lines, the wait and most of the hassle. These services allow you to either pick up the resulting prints at the store or have them delivered through postal mail. Submitting photos electronically can be a convenient option if you plan on doing a lot of editing of the images (to crop, or correct for colours, etc) before getting them printed. You can choose between various services, such as Kodak/Ofoto, Black's, Yahoo! Photos and Shutterfly, with more options to choose from and better pricing as long as you're willing to work strictly online.

Home printing

Another convenient option, which can yield professional looking results, is to simply print photos at home. Fortunately, many standard printers have entered the market combining both everyday use with specialized photo printing capabilities, for example the Canon Pixma or the HP Photosmart. If you choose to print photos at home on a colour inkjet, be sure to use the specialized photo printing paper, as that can have a big impact on the final result – with the right equipment, there can be little difference between printing at home and printing using professional traditional photo printing services.

Types of printers

To really get the most out of printing photos at home, there are specialized photo printers such as Sony's Digital Photo Printer that can both connect directly to the camera or to your PC, and use a specialized printing process that is similar to what the professionals use in photo labs. The cost per print is higher than what you would see with a multi-purpose colour printer, however, the end result is of far higher quality and will last longer, with the convenience of printing whatever photos you want, on the spot, at any time.

Sharing Photos

One of the greatest conveniences of digital cameras is being able to easily share photographs after you've taken them. Your options are almost as varied as the kinds of cameras you can choose, so you can be sure your favorite memories are seen. A tip on how to have the greatest impact with your photo albums is to resist the tendency to show every picture you've taken. With digital cameras having fewer space limitations, you often end up with several similar shots, so trimming out the duplicates will ensure that your friends and family will only see the best and most memorable shots. When you want to email pictures to friends, you can hand over the top few pictures that you really like, and archive the larger collection on your computer.

Digital photo albums

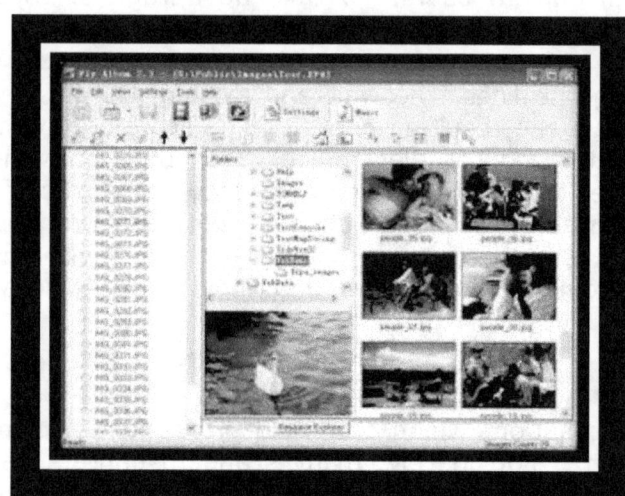

After a big trip, you can collect all your pictures and group them all in one directory or folder on your computer's hard drive – one folder for each trip will keep your pictures nicely organized. There are also a variety of software packages available (such as Google's Picasa, Apple's iPhoto or LView) to help you organize your photos, enter captions, search through the stored photos by date or caption, and do a number of simple editing adjustments - this allows you to use your computer as a digital photo album.

Online photo albums

Another option is to use one of many online photo album sites or your own website to display your photo albums online. You can either add photos to your own galleries that you create, or you can use one of these online services (such as Flickr, PBase, Kodak EasyShare Gallery, or smugmug) to your advantage, which may charge a monthly usage fee to offset storage and bandwidth costs. The advantage of using an online service is that they will optimize your picture sizes, provide storage and bandwidth, and provide photo album organization software of your pictures.

Television viewing

Another great way of sharing digital photos is to display slideshows directly using your television. There are a variety of ways to do this, including directly connecting your camera to the TV using a docking station (normally using standard RCA or S-Video cables), displaying via a laptop and connecting the laptop to your TV, or using an integrated memory card slot if your televisions provides it (some larger projection, LCD and plasma televisions provide the option of displaying photos directly off of a memory stick). This can be a great way of sharing images with larger audiences - not to mention helping to break the ice at parties.

www.ingramcontent.com/pod-product-compliance
Lightning Source LLC
Chambersburg PA
CBHW081250170526
45165CB00009B/3268